The Biscuit Joint

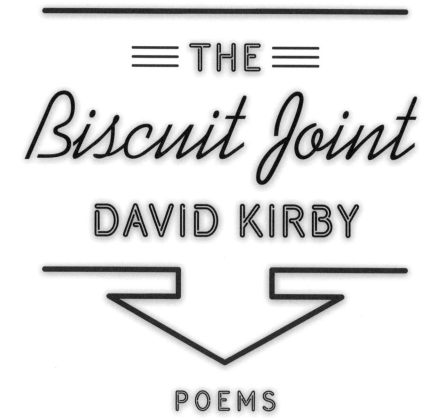

THE
Biscuit Joint
DAVID KIRBY

POEMS

LOUISIANA STATE UNIVERSITY PRESS
BATON ROUGE

Published by Louisiana State University Press
Copyright © 2013 by David Kirby
All rights reserved
Manufactured in the United States of America
First printing

Designer: Barbara Neely Bourgoyne
Typefaces: News Gothic, display; Ingeborg, text
Printer: McNaughton & Gunn, Inc.
Binder: Dekker Bookbinding, Inc.

Library of Congress Cataloging-in-Publication Data

Kirby, David, 1944–
   [Poems. Selections]
   The Biscuit Joint : poems / David Kirby.
      p. cm.
   Includes bibliographical references.
   ISBN 978-0-8071-5106-8 (cloth : alk. paper) — ISBN 978-0-8071-5107-5 (paper : alk. paper) —
   ISBN 978-0-8071-5108-2 (pdf) — ISBN 978-0-8071-5109-9 (epub) — ISBN 978-0-8071-5110-5
   (mobi)
   I. Title.
   PS3561.I66B57 2013
   811'.54—dc23
                                                                              2012043385

Many thanks to the editors of the following journals, where versions of these poems first appeared: *Arts and Letters:* "Almost Happy"; *Ecotone:* "Breathless," "Ode to My Hands," and "What's the Plan, Artists?"; *Five Points:* "Ten Thousand Hours with You"; *Hanging Loose:* "East of the Sun, West of the Moon," "I ♥ Hot Moms," and "My Favorite Foreign Language"; *Missouri Review:* "If Any Man Have an Ear, Let Him Listen," "Senior Coffee," and "Siberia"; *Ploughshares:* "Baby Handle"; *Poetry International:* "To Everyone Who Has Died Since I Was Born"; *Prairie Schooner:* "Backwards Man"; *Southern Review:* "Psychodynamic Electrohelmet," "Roy G. Biv," "The Voice in the Other Room," and "Why I Don't Drink Before Poetry Readings"; *Washington Square Review:* "Horrible Things May Be True."

For Jeanne Leiby, 1964–2011

Editor, *The Southern Review,* 2008–2011

. . . .

Jeanne was editor of *TSR* for only three years, but during that time she published eight poems of mine. Better yet, every time Jeanne saw me, she'd throw her arms around my neck and say, "You're my favorite poet." I'm sure she said this to other people—I hope she did, because a writer can hear no sweeter words. All writers want to use craft and invention to persuade the reader that their world is the real world; that's what these poems are about, and it's why I dedicate this book to her.

CONTENTS

The Biscuit Joint

WHY I DON'T DRINK BEFORE POETRY READINGS

Because it's as though even a single drop of alcohol
          awakens some area of your brain in which a thought
will begin to take shape the way a mushroom appears
               on your lawn after a heavy rainstorm: one second
      and it's not there, another and it is, though in this case
the thing that is growing in that new area of your brain
        is a phrase you've never heard before,
never even thought of, yet now you're just a heartbeat away

from saying something that no one will understand, not even
          the you who is saying it, yet you know these new words
are on their way to your mouth, that soon you will be saying
             something stupid and almost certainly offensive
      because not only has the new area of your brain opened up
and the words started to take shape in it but you
        can tell there's also a kind of conduit forming, like
a piece of plumber's pipe that leads through your forehead

and behind your nose until it opens up somewhere in the back
        of your throat, where, thanks to some
neuromuscular or chemical process or maybe one that has to do
         with the glands or the autonomic
nervous system, the phrase which left that heretofore
unknown phrase-making area of your brain at a point in time that
        now seems so distant to you, like
the moment when the first man stood up on his legs in the Pleistocene

Era or made the first ceramic pots in the Neolithic,
        has moved steadily since, like a glacier leaving
the ice banks of Greenland and bobbling among
           the other, smaller pieces of ice and the whitecaps
     as it makes its inexorable way toward the shipyards
of Nova Scotia, or, perhaps more appropriately,
        it's chugging along like a little choo-choo train leaving
Manassas Junction, say, or Tchefuncte and heading

for a big city like Chattanooga or Richmond
        or Wilmington, Delaware, only now that phrase
has changed, is now all but unholy, has turned into

something so horrible that you'll be lucky if anyone
who hears it ever speaks to you again, though that is no more
going to stop you from saying it than is
            the fact that the dean's wife is sitting in the back
of the room with several members of her book club,

wealthy women who are donors or at least potential
                donors to your university, your department, your creative
writing program, this reading series, and there they are
                    in the back, and several of them are beaming at you
        approvingly, certain that you are about to uplift
and inspire them with your version of the best that
            has been said and thought in the entirety of Western
culture, just as your university's vice president

for community affairs is beaming at you, though
            from the front row, not the back, where she is sitting
with her daughters, two adorable girls of approximately
                eight and six years of age, and the eight-year-old
        is playing a video game, though her sister
is looking around at the room, at the other people, at you,
            not quite certain why she is there
or what to expect, whether you'll deliver a homily or produce

a musical instrument and play it and sing,
            has no idea that you are about to look at the far corners
of the room, the one to the left where the bar is
                and then the other one, where the unused folding
        chairs are stacked, and take a deep breath and let half
of it out and look down at your pages and then up again
            and open your mouth and say,
"Thank you, thank you so much for that lovely introduction."

The world I tried to show was a world I would feel good in, where people would be kind, where I would find the affection that I wanted for myself. My photos were a sort of proof that such a world could exist.

—Robert Doisneau

BISCUIT JOINT: a method of creating a snug fit between two pieces of wood. The mechanics of a biscuit joint are hidden, making this technique popular for applications where wood-workers do not want people to be able to see the joint. Done right, the joint is stronger than the wood itself.

—*The Complete Woodworker's Bible*

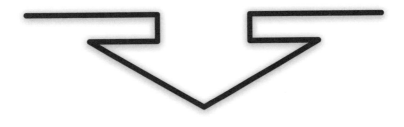

EAST OF THE SUN, WEST OF THE MOON

Friend of my mother comes up at her funeral (my mother's,
      not the friend's) and says my mom once told her that
"when David was a baby, he always seemed to be smiling,
         and I wanted to find out if he smiled all the time or began
    to smile because he heard me coming, but I never could,"
though since I was sans words in those days, I wouldn't
      know, either, would I, though it goes without saying that
    I'd like to have thrown a net over my infant experiences

and tamed them so they'd sleep by the fire on a winter's
      night, waiting for me to nudge them with a muddy boot
and come to life again and bring me out of myself as
      I sit there like the peasant in a fairy tale my mother
    used to read to me called "East of the Sun, West
of the Moon," which begins with a peasant who has
      a daughter "so lovely there was no end to her loveliness,"
    and one evening, while the family is sitting around

"busy with this thing and that," a white bear taps on
      the window, and when the peasant opens it, says
"Good evening to you," and the man says, "The same
      to you," and I was probably surprised, not that the bear
    spoke, but that the peasant didn't seem to be dumbstruck
at a bear who not only spoke fluent . . . Norwegian,
      I guess, but was also exceedingly polite, because I was
    still a child, remember, and hadn't read John Gardner's

On Becoming a Novelist and didn't know that the standards
      for good fiction included "creation of a vivid and continuous
dream, authorial generosity, intellectual and emotional
      significance, elegance and efficiency, and strangeness"—
wait, no, I *wouldn't* have been surprised, because everything
is normal to a baby since he hasn't had enough experience
      to distinguish between the normal and the ab-. So when
    Henry James was a little boy, a cousin comes to the James

house in Albany with the first installment of *David Copperfield,*
      and Henry is sent to bed because his mother thinks a reading
might not be appropriate for a little fellow, so the cousin

begins to read aloud, imitating all the voices, but as she
　　is reading about the cruelty of the Murdstones to young David,
sobs of sympathy are heard from a corner of the room,
　　　　where young Henry has hidden himself and is listening but
　　has snapped under the strain—this from Colm Tóibín's

The Master, a novel yet one that's well-researched,
　　　　and therefore the story's probably true, or at least as true
as the fairy tale in which the bear persuades the peasant
　　　　　　to give him his daughter, and they go to the bear's castle,
　　and every night a man, who is really the bear, comes
and lies down beside her, and of course she wants to get
　　　　a look at him, but she drops hot tallow on him from her candle,
　　and he starts up to say now he must marry a princess

"with a nose three yards long" who lives in a castle "east
　　　　of the sun and west of the moon," and off he goes,
but the brave girl hitches a ride on the back of the north wind, and when
　　　　　　she reaches the castle, the man or bear is there,
　　though as a prince, whom she can't wait to see, so some
captured Christians tell the prince that they hear a woman at night,
　　　　trying to wake him. Realizing what's up,
　　the prince who used to be a bear sets the princess the task of washing

the tallow from his shirt, but the spots just get bigger,
　　　　and then her mother, who is a troll, tries, and then the whole
troll family, but when the peasant girl washes the shirt,
　　　　　　the spots come out at once, and the old troll woman
　　flies into such a rage she explodes on the spot, and the princess
with the long nose after her, and the whole pack of trolls
　　　　after her, and the prince and peasant girl set
　　the Christians free and take the silver and gold and fly away forever

from "the castle that lay east of the sun and west of the moon,"
　　　　making the story certainly something less than a transcript
of what went on during my babyhood that I can't remember
　　　　　　or even a substitute for it but more like what Claude
　　Lévi-Strauss calls either "an alternative world of objective
reality" or "an objective world of alternative reality,"
　　　　a phrase I'm certain I read once but haven't
　　been able to track down since, not that it matters in that both

versions amount to the same thing, really, and may be
      the truest truth we have, because as I think about this
wonderful fairy tale that I loved so much as a child and still do
            and dip again into Colm Tóibín's *The Master,*
    I read that—holy moly!—when James's brother Wilkie
was a baby in his crib, his mother remembered that
            "he always seemed to be smiling, and she wanted to find
    out if he smiled all the time or began to smile only

because he heard her coming, but she never could."
      Do all mothers have this experience? Or did either
my mother or her friend read either a book she couldn't
            have, since it hadn't been published at the time of
    my mother's death as well as the date on which her friend
told me the story, or else the original source material
            on which Colm Tóibín based this passage, assuming he
    didn't make it up? Also, what is moly and why is it holy.

PSYCHODYNAMIC ELECTROHELMET

Fellows, it's happened to us all: you're having
            a glass of wine with a beautiful woman at an outdoor
                        café, and the weather's nice, sunny and cool but not too,
and she's wearing this floral-print dress, and one
                        of the straps keeps sliding down her arm, and she keeps
            putting it back on her shoulder but finally
decides just to let it lie there, and you're feeling pretty sexy, pretty

happy about the way things are going and confident
            that they're going to get better, when suddenly her eyes
                        roll up in her head and she says, "Some people are
doorways to other worlds." What are you going to do
                        at times like this other than give mad love and props
            to whoever came up with the phrase, "What are you
going to do?" Why, just the other day, I was putting out the trash,

and my neighbor Richard walks by with his wife Kim,
            and as I'm lowering the bag into the bin, Richard looks
                        up and says, "Nice trash," and I'm thinking, Richard
doesn't know a thing about my trash, and then I realize
                        he's just making small talk, is trying to be nice himself.
            I say there's a lot to be said for niceness,
especially in light of all the stupidity out there: this morning

in the paper, it said that masterpieces are always being
            stolen not because there's a Dr. No paying top dollar
                        for Manets and Picassos to hide away on his secret island
but because art thieves *think* there's a Dr. No paying
                        top dollar for Manets and Picassos to hide away
            on his secret island. See, the art thieves have
forgotten their Plato, who says, in the *Phaedrus,* that we must

carve nature at its joints, that is, that the world is made of parts
            that divide cleanly when we're thinking right,
                        though when we're not, we're like drunk butchers swinging
blindly at a carcass, our dull choppers bouncing off sinew
                        and bone. But you can't stop people from having ideas,
            especially wrong ones. Where do we go when we
leave this earth? On the shore of tiny Aldeburgh, on the coast

of Suffolk, I saw a war memorial that said, "They who
            this monument commemorate were numbered among
                        those who, at the call of king and country, left all
that was dear to them, endured hardship, faced danger,
                and finally passed out of the sight of men."
            Where's that, though? In a dream once, I was wearing my
psychodynamic electrohelmet, which is like a fifties football helmet

with a single-bar face mask and an electric cord with a plug
            you stick into a wall socket. My psychodynamic electrohelmet
                        would have explained everything to me, but I never got
to use it. I was at my parents' house even though I was
                        the age I am now, whereas they were younger than me even
            though they're my parents and have themselves passed
from the sight of men. And then I was in France.

And then the dream was out west somewhere, though
            this time I wasn't in it anymore, just a lot of cowboys,
                    and some had clown noses while others wore tutus.
My psychodynamic electrohelmet would be a miracle
                of rare device, and with it I would build a pleasure dome,
            sunny but with caves of ice, and a beautiful woman
there, and honeydew, and I'd drink the cherry cola of Paradise.

THE VOICE IN THE OTHER ROOM

The woman in room 1027 says, "Oh, God!"
   over and over, and I, who am in 1026, think,
Good for you, darling, until I realize that she
   is crying out in pain, not ecstasy, and that there
     are two others with her, a second woman who
murmurs, "There, there" from time to time

but also "Oh, come on, get over yourself" as well
   as a man whose words I can't make out, so low
is the timbre of his voice as well as its volume—
   why, it might as well be the voice of Whitman
     or Ginsberg oozing up through the fissures
of the earth, or that of Blake, say, or before him,

Euripides, whose dithyrambs speak of things
   more wonderful and terrible than mere heartbreak:
a woman burned to a cinder by the god who is
   her lover, a god who stitches another into his thigh,
     a king torn to pieces by his own mother, a mother
driven mad by a god. "It's so good to hear your voice!"

people say when you call them, but what does
   that mean? Some widows leave their husbands'
voices as the phone message, but the tape
   of my father reading Chaucer brings me to tears,
     the way old photos do: he was so handsome then,
so slim, and his hair was dark, and then he got old

and white-haired and, if not fat, then thick-waisted
   and slow in pace the way old men are.
In Florence once, the Arab men in the apartment below ours began
   to argue, and one slapped the other, and I braced
     myself for a fight, but there was only silence,
and then the one who was slapped started to cry.

When we bought our house, the house next door
   was occupied by three "old maids," as Colonel Donovan,

our neighbor on the other side, called them,
             and before that, by three other old maids, one of whom
                          taught at Wesleyan College in Macon, and one of her
students there was Soong Mei-ling, whose parents

had sent her to the States to be educated,
             and once she came to Tallahassee to have her teeth
worked on by her teacher's dentist but later returned
             to China and married Chiang Kai-Shek,
                          generalissimo of the army and U.S. ally
in World War II, though later he lost to the communists. It's said

that Soong spoke English with a Southern accent,
             and sometimes when I'm in my backyard listening
to the owls in the wood, I wonder what
             it would be like to hear the voice of the slender
                          Chinese girl who went on
to become the Dragon Lady, one of the world's

most powerful women, though in those days she stood under
             this oak tree I can touch with my hand, her jaw swollen,
and wondered if she'd ever see China again.
             The opening of Cole Porter's "Night and Day," a girl
                          in an attic listening
to the rain, a boy at his violin: the world taps its key,

and out come the dots and dashes,
             the grief and the love, the bad news or good news or both,
the poem that is written every day if we're there
             to read it. The next night, I hear the woman
                          in 1027 again, and she is with a different man,
a high-voiced fellow, and there are murmurs at first,

then humming, gasping, sighs, their voices together
             making chords almost, like an orchestra tuning up,
then more and louder, and at the moment of delight,
             the woman utters her joy: "Oh, God!"
                          she cries, and it's a hymn of praise
this time: "Oh, God! Oh, God! Oh, Jesus! Oh, Jesus! Oh, God!"

WHAT'S THE PLAN, ARTISTS?

Freeman Dyson said Paul Dirac's papers on quantum mechanics
were like "exquisitely carved marble statues falling out of the sky,
one after another."

        People yawn in picture galleries the way
      they do nowhere else, and I'm not talking
about some old bastard with an enlarged prostate gland
        but a pretty girl, one whose mother
      surely taught her to cover her mouth,
yet now that same orifice is open so wide and for so long that

        you wonder why an entire tribe of cave people
      hasn't set up camp in it, started cooking fires,
daubed the walls with likenesses of bison
        and tiger, and just when you think
      she can't get it open any wider,
she does, her chops racheting like the jaws of an adjustable

        wrench, and for a second you fear that she'll inhale
      and that all the art in that gallery, that city, the whole
world will disappear into her maw, which she'll
        close with an audible click and then look around
      as though to say, What just happened?
What if there were no art in the world, no books, no people

        smarter or more accomplished than our unworthy
      selves? Why, we'd have to start again, but how?
"Either plagiarism or revolution."—Gauguin.
        Easy for you to say, Paul!
      Most of us do what we do because it seems
like the right thing to do, as when Karl Marx observed that

        "Milton produced *Paradise Lost* for the same
      reason that a silk worm produces silk. It was an activity
of his nature." And when I read that music critic
        Ben Ratliff wrote that "the future belongs to those
      who can work slight variations on fixed roles,"
immediately I think of Giotto: in the Uffizi, you leave

Cimabue's *Madonna and Child Enthroned,*
which is beautiful and majestic yet flat as all
get-out, the central figures and the saints
and angels stacked on one another like place mats
at a roadside diner devoted more
to the Church's dramatis personae than to three-alarm chili

and tuna melts, and you move on to Giotto's work
of the same name, and each of his subjects seems
to stand in a separate space, that is, to have
a fully dimensional humanity, even
though they aren't human. As any nursing mother would,
Giotto's Madonna has a full bosom, but mainly there's

that right knee that all but pops out of the canvas,
signaling bodily fullness, the first in Western
portraiture; the angels at her feet look at her admiringly,
and the one on the right especially seems
to be thinking, That's some knee.
Poor Giotto: no doubt his patrons praised him for his ability

to render the likenesses of creatures they had never seen,
whereas all he wanted them to say was, "Great knee,
Giotto!" and "Now that's what I call a knee."
A few blocks away, a Michelangelo statue
of a prisoner in the Accademia convinces you that people
are really like that, but then you look at the ones

around you—the greasy-haired kid in
the FUBAR t-shirt, the bearded guy whacking his gum
as though he's getting paid for every spitty crackle,
even the big-hipped Spanish woman in tight jeans
you imagine yawning and coming
to wakefulness, her breasts spilling to the side as she raises

her hand against the day's first light—and you think,
No, people aren't that beautiful at all,
not that well-proportioned, that tragic in the way they push
against the flesh they're trapped in,
and for a moment you're angry at the lady who reminds you
of someone you knew in high school, at the serious

fellow who looks as though he just thought
of something amusing, at yourself.
What's real here, and what just looks that way?
When I talk to composer Carlisle Floyd
about *Peter Grimes,* Carlisle says
Britten's storm music does the best job of evoking a storm

without relying on musical illustration,
and when I ask what that is,
Carlisle says, "Music that sounds like a storm!"
just as Seamus Heaney warns that if you
shoehorn something into a poem,
sometimes you end up more aware of the shoehorn

than the heel. So what's the plan, artists?
First, follow "the mighty dead,"
as Keats calls them: "For us musicians," says Franz
Liszt, "Beethoven's work is
like the pillar of cloud and fire which guided
the Israelites through the desert—a pillar of cloud to guide us

by day, a pillar of fire to guide us by night,"
than which truer words have never been
spoken, though certainly funnier ones have, and if you want
funny, there's no one with
more of that admirable trait than the Henry
Fielding who says "we moderns are to the ancients

what the poor are to the rich," so that "Homer,
Virgil, Horace, Cicero, and the rest
are to be esteemed among us writers as so many wealthy
squires, from whom we, the poor
of Parnassus, claim an immemorial custom
of taking whatever we can come at." Ha, ha! Well played,

Henry! What a nut. There's no bigger nut than
Shakespeare, though, who followed all those
great tragedies with *Cymbeline,* which includes the
descent of Jupiter on an eagle, tossing thunderbolts
that knock the Ghosts to their knees.
Hokey? Sure! Obvious? You betcha! Overly theatrical?

Not by half, as the English say! But a kid would like
it, just as a kid would like "Tutti Frutti"
and "Don't You Just Know It" and "Ooh Poo Pah Doo"
and "Jock-A-Mo," songs driven by nonsense lyrics
which express the simple pleasures
of living. "They're childlike songs," says the Cosimo Matassa

who produced them all in his little studio
on the corner of Dauphine and Rampart Streets
in New Orleans; "you can imagine children
or adults dancing and skipping, finger-popping,"
because these are "expressions of joy."
Joy: now there's a word to charm magic casements.

Why, look, here's the world again! It didn't go
anywhere, after all. Or if it did, it came back,
more beautiful than it was before. Sweet old world, like
a pretty girl's breath filling an entire picture gallery
or mist on the meadow as the sun comes up
or Hamlet's father's ghost or a marble statue, falling from heaven.

TEN THOUSAND HOURS WITH YOU

Nobody in our adorable little one-horse town
knows whether *Turandot* is pronounced with
    a long or short "o" or if the "t" is voiced or silent,
        so I write opera critic Anthony
Tommasini at the *New York Times,* and he says that the vast

    majority of people in the opera world
pronounce the character's name as "TuranDOT,"
        like "spot," and I think, now there's a good fellow,
            courteous, well-informed, not so full of himself
that he can't write to a country mouse like me,

    and so I post his reply as a Facebook status update,
and you'd think that'd settle it, that the opera lovers
        of Tallahassee would let go of their plow handles
            and wipe their sweaty brows with their bandanas
and say, "Well, looky here, Ma, this newspaper

    feller says he knows how to pronounce it, and he
ought to know, him being Eye-talian and all,"
        but no, my update hasn't been on-line for more
            than fifteen seconds before someone writes
that Puccini scholar Patrick Vincent Casali

    has written an article in which he says that
"the current practice of sounding the final 't'
        of Turandot's name is incorrect," and the next
            thing you know, people are weighing in as though
Anthony Tommasini and I hadn't settled the whole

    thing just minutes before, but that's
human nature for you, isn't it? In study after study,
        researchers have established something they call
            the Ten Thousand Hours Rule, which says that's
how long it takes to get really good at something—

    cello playing, archery, poetry, safecracking, chess,
you name it—and therefore you should expect to put in

about twenty hours a week over a period of ten years
before you're an expert. Then again, most of us have
spent more time than that in cars, yet we still drive

the wrong way on freeways, cross into the other guy's
lane while texting, careen off cliffs, and, if we are
James Dean or Jayne Mansfield, get hit head-on
by 23-year-old Cal Poly student Donald Turnupseed
or plow into the rear of a semi that had slowed

because of a truck spraying mosquito fog, prompting
the National Highway Traffic Safety Administration
to require an "underride guard" on all tractor-trailers
to minimize the damage of future mishaps. When you
come right down to it, we do our best or think we do,

which amounts to the same thing: historian Doug
Blackmon tells me that half of Thomas Jefferson
and Sally Hemings' kids looked like her and stayed on
at Monticello as slaves, whereas the ones who looked
like TJ "ran away and became white people," so that

today there are hundreds of thousands of white folks
out there who are (a) black and (b) Thomas Jefferson's
descendants, though they don't know it, and now they're
doing yoga and drinking designer coffee
and going to Wes Anderson movies, and they don't really like any

of this, but they have to do it because they're white.
To me, New York is the place where people know
how to pronounce every word correctly, seeing
as how every language group is represented there,
although not even New Yorkers can manage "Houston

Street." Or a New Yorker might want to say
"I'm right," for example, and have it come out "I'm white,"
which isn't the same thing. Or what if I called you "belle"
and you thought I called you "bel" (the Indian thorn tree)
or "Bel" (the Babylonian god)? I'd like to say everything

to you and say it right. Imagine yourself sitting next to me
on the subway, either in New York or just in your mind.
I might be the great-great-grand-something
of a U.S. president, you know. I'll lean over
and say "beauty" to you, and you'll look at me and say "beast."

I ♥ HOT MOMS

The guy with the "I ♥ Hot Moms" t-shirt makes his way
down the airplane aisle, and I think, who doesn't?
Hot moms even ♥ themselves, or we wouldn't see so many
of them in groups of five or six at your finer restaurants,
laughing and getting drunk while, back home, their kids text
and bully each other and wait for their hot moms to return
and help them with their assignments, and their morose

husbands stare into their computer screens at stock prices
or sports scores or hot-mom porn sites. Therefore what
profiteth it a young man to declare his affection for
these inestimable women, these fleshy beauties whose
maiden years are behind them yet whose lives as crones
are ahead of them by a multiple of, say, two. Why,
it's as though you're saying you like babies or kittycats

or that, given the choice, you'd rather eat ice cream
than hog vomit mixed with mud. How slender the line
between our thoughts, so virginal, so uncomplicated,
and the world into which those thoughts step, so ungainly
now, so cumbrous and bunglesome. At the symphony
once, I strolled about during the interval and returned
to find a young gentleman in the row behind ours with

his elbows on the back of my seat, and he was saying
something to Barbara that I couldn't hear, and she said
something to him, and the people around them roared
with laughter. "What was that about?"
I say, and Barbara tells me the young fellow asked her if she'd
like to go out sometime, and she says, No, thank you,
I'm married, and he says, Too bad—I like older

women, and she says, You need to work on your lines,
and that's what sets off our neighbors, all of whom
are a lot closer to our ages than his. Young men,
young men! You must be like Jude in the Hardy novel,
who, on first discovering his intellectual powers,
"ran about and smiled outwardly at his inward thoughts,
as if they were people meeting and nodding to him—

smiled with that singularly beautiful irradiation which
is seen to spread on young faces at the inception
of some glorious idea, as if a supernatural lamp were held
inside their transparent natures, giving rise to the flattering
fancy that heaven lies about them." Let the hot moms
of your imagination descend as from paradise to flirt
with and caress you; let them lift their shirts over their

heads and toy with your belt buckle and in that way light
you from within, guiding you to better choices in, say, casual
wear—a tailored shirt open at the throat, cuffs
turned back twice—or in the type of remark that doesn't
end conversations but begins them, like "I'm glad they're
playing work by contemporary composers, aren't you?"
and "How did Beethoven do it? He couldn't hear a thing!"

And it was about then, about that time, that I began to find life unsatisfactory as an explanation of itself and was forced to adopt the method of the artist of not explaining but putting the blocks together in some other way that seems more significant to him.

—Tennessee Williams

I don't really have any goals as a songwriter other than to show what it's like to be a person—just like everybody else who's ever played music does.

—Elliott Smith

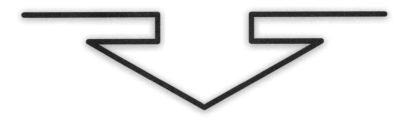

BACKWARDS MAN

Dennis O'Driscoll is in the National Gallery at the moment
        looking at the Titians with another Irish poet, and this one
is Seamus Heaney, who seems destined to be not only

    the first Noble Laureate I've encountered but also, unless
        Toni Morrison plops herself in my lap and ruffles my hair
and tells me how adorable I am, the last, and he, too, is as sweet

    as he can be—"full of sermons-on-the-mount," as Melville
        said of Shakespeare, "and gentle, aye, almost as Jesus"—
and in this fashion do the three of us, the two genial

    and self-assured Irish poets and the American one,
        begin to talk not of poetry or the weather but the circuses
they'd seen as boys, with Dennis saying that often the person

    who tore tickets bore more than a passing resemblance
        to the sword swallower, just as the lady on the tightwire
seemed very like the one who sold candy floss during

    the interval, but when I ask them if their Irish circuses
        featured sideshows of the kind I saw in the American South,
they say, "No, no," and when I say, "No Bearded Lady, then,

    no Camel Girl, Human Unicorn, Three-Legged Boy?" they say,
        "No, no, David, nothing like that," which should be enough
of a signal to me to move on to Renaissance portraiture

    or the fragile truce in Ireland or any of the hundred subjects
        I could discuss with these kindly and learned gentlemen,
though my nervousness begins to play the part of the bullying

    schoolmaster to the reluctant schoolboy that is my stupidity
        yet who knows enough to stay in the wings and not butcher
the tune or the lines it hasn't mastered, but no, no, the pedagogue

    will have his way, and so I begin to babble about the clowns,
        the elephants who were so sad and so incontinent,
the marvelous food—the kettle corn, elephant ears, funnel cakes, fried dill

pickles, and, best of all, the corn dog, than which there is no
              delicacy more sublime—though mainly I'm banging on
about Backwards Man, the freak who frightened

me most, because he wore a ratty bathrobe and stood
              in profile and began to speak in an awful voice
as he turned in a half circle from the ankles up, finally

facing in the opposite direction, even though his toes
              still pointed forward. And when you're a kid, when
everybody's first question to you is, "What're ya

going to be when ya grow up, young fella!" you can't
              help but wonder, What if I grow up to be Backwards
Man and spend my days contorting myself before

gaggles of horrified schoolchildren, standing there
              with their stomachs sticking out and their buck teeth
and looking at you as though you're some kind

of monster, which you are, though the worst thing
              about you is that horrible voice, that drone of despair
into which all happiness vanishes, all light, joy,

beauty. And who will love the Backwards
              Man that is you? Can you imagine having sex
if you're backwards? Not that a certain *contrapposto*

isn't desirable: why, just upstairs in this same
              gallery is one of the most erotic paintings in the world,
Bronzino's *Allegory with Venus and Cupid,*

in which little-boy Cupid is crouched slightly behind
              yet twisting back toward the naked goddess whose
saucy nipple peeps between his splayed fingers,

and she seems as though she's on the verge of slipping
              her tongue into his mouth, and you can't tell whether
he's turning toward her with lust or away from her

in repugnance, because it's his mother, for Christ's
        sake, although, for all that, this is the kissiest art work
any artist has ever produced, kissier by far than any

    statue by Canova or Rodin, indeed, so kissy
        that it makes me think of the poem by Catullus
in which he says, "Give me a thousand kisses,

    then a hundred, / Then another thousand,
        then a second hundred, / Then, constantly, another
thousand, then a hundred, / Then, when we will have

    done that many thousands of times, / We will confuse
        the count, so that we ourselves
don't know." Seamus Heaney says there are three kinds

    of poetry: civic, public, and political, and of these,
        I think I must be writing the first kind
and therefore am a civic poet, if not the kind that, say, Auden is,

    going on about how people and cultures develop and interact
        with each other as well as an uncaring
natural world, but another kind altogether. I'm the poet of circuses

    but also art galleries and snacks. Really, though, I'd like to be
        the poet of kindness and learning. Oh,
and kisses! And encounters, of course—chance encounters.

ROY G. BIV

The English say "Richard Of York Gave Battle In Vain"
        when they try to recall the colors of the rainbow,
    but that assumes a sense of history, which we Americans
don't like so much. What we like is sports, even soccer,
        but what does Greg O'Keeffe of *The Liverpool*
Echo mean when he describes forward Landon

Donovan's "coruscating pace down the flanks"?
        Well, "pace," yeah, but "flank" is a steak in this country,
    and "coruscating" never even made it through customs!
Some mnemonics are funner than the things they remind
        you of, such as "Kids Prefer Cheese Over Fried Green
Spinach," that is, the order of taxonomy in biology—

kingdom, phylum, class, et cetera—which is helpful when
        you're trying to understand Darwin, but only half of us
    believe in him. And some are so confusing! Take
"Red on black, friend of Jack / Red on yellow, kill
        a fellow." Or is it "Black on red, you'll soon be
dead." Or "You heard what I said." Maybe it's "Red

on black, you're on the right track," though
        by the time you remember, you've either been killed
    by the eastern coral snake or had a heart attack
as the Florida scarlet snake slithers harmlessly away.
        No, I'm going with Roy G. Biv, because I think that
would make a great name for an American poet,

one whose dog wants to know why men look at women
        the way they do. Also, why have y'all messed
    up the environment, and no heaven for dogs—now why's
that? This poet's high school teacher would
        bring to class a picture of her sister, who has just won
the lottery, and tear it up and give every student

a piece of the torn photo. He'd write poems with
        titles like "Are Nudists Nuts?"—*the* question
    of our time, to my way of thinking—and lines

like "We approve of intersections but are opposed
          to streets" and "Out with mayors, in with majordomos"
and "We have too many potholes. They should be

filled with violets or ideas." Let me be the Emerson
          of our day, and let me say to our national poet,
     not "Thou shalt have the whole land
for thy park and manor, the sea for thy bath and navigation,"
          but "Thou shalt go over to thy friend's
house to play and end up looking out a storm door

on a snowy day while thy friend shoots baskets
          outside and, seated behind thee, his mother
     gets quietly drunk, and in that way shalt thou learn despair"
and "Thou shalt be sent as a boy by thy mother
          to fetch thine older sister, who is making out
with some guy in a car, and thou shalt watch them

for a minute as they swap slow, dreamy kisses,
          and thou shalt creep away silently, and in that way
     shalt thou learn privacy." Look! It's late at night,
and a truck idles at a loading dock, and
          there's Roy G. Biv, and he's thinking of the types
of cranial nerves and trying to remember which

are sensory, which motor, and which both, and he
          says to himself, "Some Say Marry
     Money, But My Brother Says Big Boobs Matter More"
but also "Some Say Marilyn Monroe, But
          My Brother Says Brigitte Bardot? Mmmm,
Mmmmm!" and even "Some Say Marry Money,

But My Brother Says 'Bitch Betta Have My Money!'"
          as he packs the truck with tchotchkes and geegaws
     and whatnots and slides each tightly into place while
we sleep in the next town over and dream
          of everything we forgot or never knew in the first place,
and we do now, or not yet, but we will, and soon.

SENIOR COFFEE

"Medium coffee," I say, and think, Hold on, I've had too much
already, so I say, "No, make it a small—wait a sec," and the counter
    guy says, "You want a senior coffee?" and I say, "No—uh, yeah!"

My first senior coffee—senior anything, really. Only 89 cents!
And not bad, either. Or not great, but as good as the coffee I was
    going to get anyway, and a lot cheaper. At home, I show Barbara

the little paper cup: "Hey, look, senior coffee." Big mistake:
after that, it's "How about a senior coffee?" and "I'm making
    coffee—you want regular coffee or senior coffee?" And soon

everything's senior. Do you have your senior cell phone with you?
Bring home a senior newspaper, will you? Those sneakers look
    a little worn; why don't you get some new sneakers—senior

sneakers. And when I say I'm bored, she says, "Why don't
you write one of those senior poems you're so famous for?"
    All poetry is senior, of course. At a party, a professor in one of

the "practical" disciplines questions the value of teaching
people to be poets, and I think, The ancients assigned three
    muses to poetry: Calliope to epic poetry, Erato to love poetry,

and Euterpe to song and elegaic poetry. How many muses
did you say you have in Design Leadership Systems?
    I wonder if there's a guy out there named Señor Poetry.

He'd be at a table in a plaza somewhere with his wife and daughter,
Señora and Señorita Poetry. He'd be drinking coffee and writing
    poems, and everyone would be looking over his shoulder.

What is he writing? Wait, wrong question. A better one is how
is he writing, since style is so much more important than
    subject matter. Henry James says a woman living in a quiet

country village has only to be "a damsel upon whom nothing is lost"
to write about soldiers and garrison life. Truer words, Henry,
    truer words! No one's more senior than Henry James.

Some onlookers are guessing that Señor Poetry is writing
in the manner of Baroque lyric poet Luis de Góngora, though
others say no, he can't be. Góngora's contemporaries called

him "the Spanish Homer" but also the inventor of "Pestilential
Poetry." Not for Góngora the poem in which language works
in the background while the story gets told. No, sir, his is

the language that steps into the footlights and windmills its arms,
which is why his fans and detractors pronounced him the greatest
of poets as well as a pretentious fool. And maybe Señor Poetry

is not a poet at all, any more than a man named Señor Smith shoes
horses for a living or one named Señor Miller owns a mill.
Maybe his wife's the poet. Or his daughter: maybe she's

Henry James's damsel upon whom nothing is lost. They're so
proud of her! I am, too. I love her as much as though she
were my daughter, which means I want her to have a life

like mine, one lived, not for poetry but through poetry.
Everything—a car starting, bird song, the gurgling
of a coffeepot, the whirr of a fan, the whispers of lovers,

the silly noises babies make, the wisdom of the books
the mighty dead have written—all of that steps easily into
poetry and makes itself at home there. Poetry and coffee:

now there's a combination for you. Though if the poetry's strong
enough, you'll need nothing more than a lifetime in which to
read and write the stuff, I think, and then I think, Famous? Me?

ALMOST HAPPY

My father is the first of our parents to die, and when
        he does, Barbara says, "We only have to do this three
    more times, right?" So many ways to do it. My dad

just told my mom that they ought to hit the road, then put
        his head on her shoulder and went to sleep. But if you
    want, you can take your own life, and that of your

pretty wife, too—when Othello kills himself, he uses
        sleight of hand to distract Lodovico, Montano, Cassio,
    and Gratiano as he readies the sword with which he will

stab himself to death and tells the story of an epic
        battle with a "malignant and turban'd Turk," ending
    the military recap and his own life at the same moment

when he says, "I took by th' throat the circumcised
        dog, / And smote him—thus." To dead Desdemona
    he says with his last breath, "I kiss'd thee ere

I kill'd thee: no way but this; / Killing myself,
        to die upon a kiss," for so mixed are love and hate
    that if we are not heedful, if we are not cautious

and sober stewards of our emotions, then we will find
        ourselves no better off than the young nobleman
    named Julian who, returning from the hunt

one day and thinking himself to have surprised
        his wife in bed with her lover, drew his sword
    and slew the covered figures, only to learn that,

in his absence, his parents had come to visit, and,
        respectful daughter-in-law that she was, his missus
    had offered the best bed in the house to the mother

and father of the now-orphaned noble who renounced
        all his worldly goods, withdrew to a river bank,
    and, as St. Julian the Poor (though not yet), devoted

the rest of his life to ferrying strangers to the other side.
        One dark and stormy night, a leprous pilgrim
    appeared and demanded to be carried over despite

the evident dangers, and, after several hesitations,
        the saint-to-be invited the stranger into his bark,
    and when they were in the middle of the river, the leper's head

became surrounded by a luminous nimbus, and it was—
        guess who, reader! That's right! Jesus Christ, come
    to take away the sins of the unhappy parricide!

And you thought you had problems. Boy, I'd feel awful
        if I'd done what Julian had, wouldn't you? Future
    sainthood notwithstanding. When I recount

some mistake or other I've made to Barbara and say,
        "At least I never killed my mom and dad," she says,
    "Well, you're okay there, Dave." But looking back,

I realize that, at the end of his life, I wanted my father
        to die, to put down the burden that had become
    himself and not drag it into his eighty-ninth year.

And I hope my own sons will feel that way
        about me, that they'll see the humor in it.
    Death: either you get it or you don't.

Conductor Lorin Maazel says, "The idea of dying
        is like a joke or a literary device. It's not all that bad.
    So you fall into eternal sleep. So what?"

Maybe that's what Henry James meant when he wrote that,
        in the hours following their mother's last moments,
    he and his brothers and sister were "almost happy."

MY FAVORITE FOREIGN LANGUAGE

"What's your favorite foreign language?" asks the cabbie,
              and when I ask why, he says he knows "butterfly"
    in 241 of them, so I say, "Okay, French!" and he says,

"*Papillon!*" and I say, "German!" and he says, "*Schmetterling!*"
              and I'm running out of languages I know, so I say,
    "Uh, Wolof!" because I'm reading a short story

where a woman speaks Wolof, and he says something in Wolof,
              and the professor-y part of me wants
    to say, You shouldn't call them foreign languages, you know,

because that means there's only one real language, but
              I'd be saying that to him in our common
    tongue, so it really wouldn't make sense unless I were chiding

him in, say, Wolof, a language in which he knows only
              one word and I none. What's the best country?
    Heaven, probably: as everyone knows, the cooks are French,

the mechanics German, the police English, lovers
              Italian, and it's all organized by the Swiss,
    whereas in Hell, the cooks are English, mechanics

French, police Germans, lovers Swiss, and everything
              is organized by the Italians.
    What about the Spanish, though? The ancients say a man should

speak French to his friends because of its vivacity, Italian
              to his mistress for its sweetness,
    German to his enemies because it is forceful, and Spanish

to his God, for it is the most majestic of languages.
              Hola, Señor! Okay if I put my suitcase
    over here? Thank you for having me! Yes, I *would*

like to hear what they're saying in the other place, like "Dictators
              over here" and "Corporate polluters
    in this area" and "Aw, come on—*another* boring poet?"

BABY HANDLE

Samurai sword-fighting lesson, Tokyo

We're using the *iaitō* or "practice sword" now
　　　　as opposed to the *shinken* or "live sword" which
looks as though it can cut through lampposts
　　　　　　　　and is "hungry for the flesh of its owner,"
says smiling Sakaguchi-san through a translator,
　　　　which is why I'm getting lots of unintentional laughs

when I keep saying, "Can we just check the edges
　　　　one more time before we start?" It's impossible
not to swagger when you're wearing a sword
　　　　　　　　and are Western, though the Japanese don't swagger;
they just scurry up to one another and start hacking.
　　　　Well, not "scurry": the idea, we learn, isn't to win,

it's to not lose, because when you're trying to win,
　　　　you're rushing in heedlessly and making all kinds
of mistakes, whereas when you're trying to not lose,
　　　　　　　　you're taking your time and waiting for your enemy
to screw up so you can exploit his error, presuming
　　　　your opponent is considerate enough to be heedless

and mistake-prone. You want to attain *heijōshin*,
　　　　in other words, which is one of those untranslatable
Japanese philosophical concepts best rendered here
　　　　　　　　as "mindfulness" and which Sakaguchi-san wants me
to have when we are sparring with the *bokken*
　　　　or "wooden sword" and I try to clobber him.

"Uh, uh!" he says, wagging his finger at me and then,
　　　　using his only English of the day, "Baby
handle. Baby handle!" And he takes my forearm and caresses it
　　　　　　　　and even puts my hand to his face and closes his eyes
as though he is putting a child to sleep. Goodnight, baby!
　　　　Sleep tightly, little Japanese baby that was once my arm

and is trying to be heedless and error-prone instead
　　　　of mindful as we change positions and Sakaguchi-san

draws his *bokken* from his *obi* and advances on me,
        and I remember how the most famous
samurai of them all, Miyamoto Musashi, once asked his disciple
           Jōtarō what his goal was, and when Jōtarō said

"To be like you!" Musashi-san replied, "Uh, uh!
        Your goal is too small! You should aspire to be like
Mount Fuji, with such a broad and solid foundation
           that nothing can move you, not even the strongest
earthquake! You will then see all things clearly:
        not just things happening near you but forces that shape

all events," and as Sakaguchi-san seizes the wooden sword
        with two hands and raises it above his head, I think
of Shakespearean actor Mark Rylance, of whom
           it's been said that he seems to have more time
than anyone else, like an athlete—like Michael
        Jordan, say, because if it takes you three seconds to shoot

a lay-up, it seems as though Jordan-san is in the air for ten
        seconds, fifteen, more. The *bokken*
in my teacher's double-handed grip has reached the end of its arc,
           and now that he's bringing it down,
I remember as well that John Berryman essay on Shakespeare
        with its recollection of *Twelfth Night* in which Laurence

Olivier as Sir Toby Belch and Alec Guinness
        as Sir Andrew Aguecheek played the drinking scenes
so slowly that, in Berryman's words, "they might almost
           have been dead," as though Hamlet himself had told
them to "speak the speech . . . trippingly in the tongue;
        but if you mouth it, as many of our players do, I had

as lief the town-crier spoke my lines. Nor do not
        saw the air too much with your hand, thus, but use all gently;
for in the very torrent, tempest, and, as I may say,
           whirlwind of your passion, you must acquire and beget
a temperance that may give it smoothness."
        Baby handle, good sirs! O for a Muse of fire

that would ascend the brightest heaven of invention!
    And were I a samurai, then at my heels, leashed in
like hounds, should famine, sword, and fire crouch
                for employment! Bang! Sakaguchi-san raps me
smartly with his *bokken,* and I realize that
        if he had been using his *shinken* or even his *iaitō,*

then my head would now be in two neat pieces.
    Banished to the sideline, I watch as he spars with another
student and see how, when the sword is falling
        on Sakaguchi-san's own head, he looks at it for what
seems like minutes, weighing his options
        until he picks the right one and then flicking

his opponent's weapon to one side as a king on a battlefield
        might unhorse another or a baby put aside his toy and take up
the crown his mother has brought him
            as she brushes back his hair and kisses him and says
Take this, wear it, and gestures toward the wide world
        behind her and says, Take this, too, it's yours.

It's like this painter who lives around here—he paints the area in a radius of twenty miles, he paints bright strong pictures. He might take a barn from twenty miles away, and hook it up with a brook right next door, then with a car ten miles away, and with the sky on some certain day, and the light on the trees from another certain day. A person passing by will be painted alongside someone ten miles away. And in the end he'll have this composite picture of something which you can't say exists in his mind. It's not that he started off willfully painting this picture from all his experience. . . . That's more or less what I do.

—Bob Dylan

I am ashamed to have spoken of my own personal case—except for the fact that people always hope for confessions and I have no reason to deny them mine.

—Jorge Luis Borges

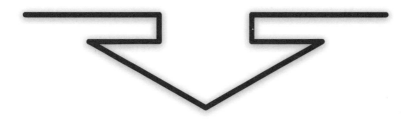

ODE TO MY HANDS

How about a quote, says our university's media rep,
who's writing a piece on Barbara, so I say I married
Barbara because I couldn't keep my hands off her,
      and the media rep says, Great! and then calls back
an hour later to say, Sorry, the boss says no, and when

      I ask why, she says it's the hands, and when somebody
says that to you, you can't help looking at your hands
and saying, Boys, it's not your fault. Think of everything
      you have done: you have changed my sons'
diapers, and, as he lay dying, my father's as well.

      You have made countless small meals for those sons
and their friends as well as an equal number of pedestrian
and occasionally fine ones for the wife who was the nominal
      topic of this poem until you displaced
her and, when that wife has been out of town, for male friends for whom

      I've fried, baked, and barbecued and with whom I've drunk
all day on my deck, during which time you turned
ribs on the grill as well as sausage links and chicken
      and lifted tots of whiskey and bottles
of beer to your confederates in bodily pleasure, my lips, and put on

      music and mopped up messes and showed those friends
to their cars and, when they have been too drunk, to bed.
You have lit both firecrackers and fine cigars. You
      have tortured successively the clarinet,
the trumpet, the piano, and now the guitar, the right hand plucking

      one string as the left presses the string either above
or below and then goes lower or higher as the right does
the opposite and another false note is struck, though a new one this time.
      You have sawed wood, hammered
nails, changed flats, and felt fire running through you that time I changed

      the electrical outlet in the kitchen and forgot to cut
the power. You bear scars: a nick on the left index finger

from a dropped pop bottle, a monkey bite on the right
                    thumb, and, next to it, an L-shaped reminder
of a chemistry experiment gone wrong. You have fired rifles, shotguns,

            and both types of pistol. You have played sports, even
        though you dropped more balls than you caught,
and buried the bodies of pets beloved and despised. To my shame,
                    though not yours, at parties you have
caressed the bottoms of friends' wives who, to their credit, turned

            in surprise and, on seeing it was me, smiled indulgently
        and went back to their conversations instead
of telling their husbands, who would have beaten
                    me with their own hands. Barbara herself has
spoken of you and, indeed, to you, praising you in terms beyond

            your merit. For you are not lovely: you are too small
        for someone my size, and your fingers are more like
sausages than the long and tapered fingers of pianists
            and cardiothoracic surgeons. When
the media rep calls to ask if it's okay to say "couldn't live without

            Barbara" instead of "couldn't keep my hands off her,"
        I can't help saying, Yeah, but that's the kind
of thing that sounds best if you say it with a fakey European
                    accent, and then I look at
you guys again. I haven't even gotten to the things to which you give

            most of your time: brushing, flossing, turning pages,
        and scratching your best friends, my other body parts.
When I finish writing about you, you'll lie quietly
                    in your favorite resting place, my lap,
and when I close you, you'll open again, as though ready to speak.

BREATHLESS

Film directed by Jean-Luc Godard, 1960, starring Jean-Paul Belmondo
and Jean Seberg; also song recorded by Jerry Lee Lewis, 1958

Jean-Paul Belmondo, I'm thinking of you tonight
because I saw you walking down the Boulevard
        St. Germain just this afternoon with a young woman,
and not a starlet, either, but a nurse, and you were
        using a cane, yet you were as handsome as you were
in all those movies you made thirty, forty, fifty

        years ago, or, if not handsome, *beau-laid,*
as the French say, or handsome-ugly, as we all are
        in our way. My students don't know who you are,
but then I don't really know who my students are
        or they me. Women love you
because you neither gaze too long into the mirror of your own

        excellence nor deny your manifest charms,
for our self-loathing may be so great as to become
        a kind of narcissism, as I see when I am
still in my own land and out shopping one day and pondering
        the tall guy in the cargo shorts and black knee socks
in the food co-op sighing as he shelves bags of Garden of Eatin'

        Black Bean Tortilla Chips while his shorter
and more stylishly attired friend is saying, "I just
        didn't want you to be the laughingstock of Tallahassee,"
and the cargo shorts guy sighs again and puts out
        more bags of tortilla chips and says, "I'm afraid
it's too late for that," and I think, now that's giving

        your unworthy self a certain stature, isn't it?
To claim to be the biggest jackass in your town,
        even if it's a small one like Tallahassee? Hee, haw!
Look at me, everybody! A jackass and loving it.
        A month earlier, I had given a reading
at Ohio University and was walking one evening along

the Ridges, the site of a deserted and terrible-looking
mental hospital, a Gothic nightmare that, though
           empty, still breathed exhaustion and despair.
The buildings looked like the mind itself: well-meaning
           but too heavy, and I was tired and had a plane to catch
and saw in the distance a couple driving along

           slowly and possibly thinking, as I was, of the good
intentions associated with this place, of the pain,
           and I wanted to ask them for a ride downhill,
and I think they would have given me one
           gladly had they known I was an English professor,
but I couldn't see myself just then, and I didn't know

           how I looked, and I don't think they would have
mistaken me for a mental patient—those had all been
           gone for years—but they might have taken me
for an actor in a horror movie set on the grounds
           of a deserted mental hospital, maybe somebody
who didn't know when to stop acting. How do you

           know when to stop? In the movies,
Jean-Paul, you were cool before "cool"
           came to mean "whatever," as when one person
says, "I can't stand the sight of you anymore,"
           and the other person says, "That's cool."
And you were "awesome" before that word was used mainly

           to describe pizza. You taught young men like me
not to be cool but to try to be, and if it never worked,
           at least our efforts won us the young women
who loved us for trying, who forgave us
           and let us think that they thought us awesome.
Jean-Paul Belmondo, you leave me breathless.

TO EVERYONE WHO HAS DIED SINCE I WAS BORN

There are so many of you! Thanks for
        coming by. No telling what the neighbors
will say, not to mention the people in Georgia,
        Alabama, and Mississippi whose front yards
        you've also filled. Or the people in the whole
world, really. How many of you are there?
        After all, you started dying when I started
breathing, one by one in your beds and then more

quickly in wars as well as mass famines,
        deliberate and otherwise. Speaking of which,
Hitler and Stalin died, too, though I don't exactly
        see them walking around among you
        and shaking hands! Why not, though?
What are you going to do, kill them again? Anyway, how
        many—wait, I can look it up
in another window, where I see the best estimate

is four billion, which sounds a little too
        good to be true, just as they say that Mount
Everest is exactly twenty-three thousand feet
        high whereas it's reported as twenty-three thousand
        and two in the reference books so the real
height won't sound like a guess. When Walt
        Whitman was between thirty-one and thirty-three,
        as he says in "A Backward Glance o'er Travel'd

Roads," a desire that had been flitting through
        his life, or hovering on the flanks, had steadily
advanced to the front and finally dominated everything,
        and this was his wish to express in poetic form
        his own physical, emotional, moral, intellectual,
and aesthetic personality while also tallying—
        and this is the money part—"the momentous
        spirit and facts of its immediate days"

and to "exploit that personality, *identified with place
        and date,* in a far more candid and comprehensive

sense than any hitherto poem or book." Emphasis
            mine! Anyway, Whitman did it, and I'm trying,
        with help from so many others: Dante, for example,
    and Shakespeare. John Donne, of course. Emily Dickinson. Anyway,
            I owe you people! I started having my fun
        about the time yours ended. Not that it's all been draft beer

        and hot fudge sundaes: I've worked hard, though most of you
            wouldn't call what I do work. And I've written
    some halfway decent poems, though none like
            the ones by my masters, and here I have
        to say that the great majority of you are lucky
    you missed out on the internet with its postings
            of whatever anybody feels like saying and, worse,
        what anybody else feels like saying back, which,

        in my case, would mean jackasses who haven't done
            a damned thing with their lives crawling all over me
    for comparing myself, which I'm so not doing,
            to those whom Keats called "the mighty
        dead." And though poetry doesn't mean anything to most
    of you, a lot of you are in those poems I wrote
            earlier, and you're all in this one. Come on
        in, Grandma! You can sit next to Federico García Lorca.

SIBERIA

I'm not thinking of vodka or the czar or the Orthodox Church
        or any other typically Russian topic
    as I look out the window of the train
between Ekaterinburg and Irkutsk but of orgies, of all things,
        which I assume occur here
    at the same rate at which orgies occur in other countries

or maybe even a slightly higher one, given
        the cold winters and general malaise
    of a people living in what is still largely
a feudal society, which doesn't mean I'm thinking
        of organizing or being in or even
    watching an orgy, in Russia or elsewhere, but how,

according to an article I'd read by a guy who'd
        been in one, they're pretty unsatisfactory,
    on the whole: the people are pasty-skinned
and dumpy, and either you can't get the others
        to do what you want to, or else you have people
    trying to get you to do something you don't want to do,

and yet the whole time the guy was excited
        because he was thinking, "I'm at an orgy!
    I'm at an orgy!" And that's the way I feel as I look out
the window and think, "I'm in Siberia!" Only
        Siberia is beautiful, not scary. The birch trees are
    so slim and silvery that you expect them to thrum

like harp strings as the wind rushes through
        their branches and tosses their green leaves
    this way and that, and there are mountains
in the distance and rivers in the foreground,
        and people are bathing in the rivers,
    Russian people, and they're laughing and splashing

each other, not starving or freezing to death
        or pulling their teeth out with their own fingers
    or being beaten by sadistic guards, which is all

you can think about when somebody says
              "Siberia" to you, but this is Siberia, and it's beautiful.
      Well, not if you're writer Varlam Shalamov

who spent seventeen years in a camp there.
              Shalamov's greatest story is "Cherry Brandy";
      in it he imagines the thoughts of the dying poet Mandelstam:
"Life entered by herself, mistress in her own
              home. He had not called her, but she entered
      his body, his brain. . . . Poetry was the lifegiving force

by which he had lived. Yes, it had been exactly
              that way. He had not lived for poetry; he had lived
      through poetry." When he was a boy, Shalamov's
father tried to stop him from reading so much:
              "Stop reading!" he'd cry, and "Put down
      that book—turn the light off!" He didn't, of course,

which is probably why he became a lover of poetry
              even if he didn't become a poet.
      And it's why he could write, in "Cherry Brandy,"
that "everything—work, the thud of horses' hoofs,
              home, birds, rocks, love, the whole world—
      could be expressed in poetry" and "each word

was a piece of the world." In his memoirs,
              Shalamov says his father never spoke to him
      of another poet, Batyushkov, and from this he concludes
that "my father did not like poetry, feared
              its dark power, far from common sense."
      He praises Batyushkov's poems for "preserving

the most unexpected discoveries" and then
              quotes a line from him: "O heart's memory,
      you are stronger than reason's sad memory."
No wonder people love poetry and the powerful
              fear it. "Poetry is respected only in this country,"
      Mandelstam said; "there's no place where more

people are killed for it." I'm not afraid of you, poetry,
              therefore I must not be powerful.

But you are. Poetry for president! Tippecanoe
and poetry, too. United we stand, divided
        we write poetry. Poetry's got my back!
    Tread on me, somebody—go ahead,

I dare you. I think a poem must be like
        an orgy—okay, you're disappointed most
    of the time, but you never know what's going
to happen. Plus you can make the people
        in your poem as handsome as movie stars.
    Why aren't we all poets? Why aren't we all in jail.

IF ANY MAN HAVE AN EAR, LET HIM LISTEN

My mother-in-law says, "You want something?" and I say,
no, I'll just work on my sand fort, so she heads for
the lunch wagon, and I'm standing on Waimanalo Beach
when I see a beast rise up out of the sea having
seven heads and ten horns, and upon his horns ten crowns, and upon

his heads the name of blasphemy, and I say, "Holy moly—
the Antichrist!" and the beast says, "Where she go?"
and I say, "My mother-in-law? She went to get a hot dog—
what do you want with her?" and the beast says, "She been
talkin. She been waitin. Here I am," but he's saying this

with all seven of his heads at the same time, so he sounds like
the Temptations, only with three extra Temps. "Those extra
voices . . . ," I start to say, but he says, "I makin war on saints,"
and I say, "My mother-in-law's no saint. I mean,
I love her and all, but go to, like, ancient Rome . . . ," and by now most

of his heads are looking at me as though he's noticed
me for the first time, so I say, "You ever read *King Solomon's
Mines* by H. Rider Haggard? Story of the elephant hunter
who goes looking for diamonds with a map
drawn in blood?" but now the beast is twisting his necks around, and half

of his heads are looking for my mother-in-law, and the other
half are sucking up water and spraying it around and slapping
against the torso of his body, and I'm guessing he's not much
of a reader, so I say, "When you popped out
of the waves, first thing I thought of was that book—actually, not the book

so much as what V. S. Pritchett wrote about it, which is that
whereas E. M. Forster said the novelist sends a bucket
down into the unconscious, Pritchett said Haggard
installed a suction pump and drained
the whole reservoir of the public's secret desires," and just as I'm about

to say "and you make H. Rider Haggard look like
a Sunday school teacher," he clambers onto the beach,

and he's got a dragon with him, and there's a woman on one
of his shoulders arrayed in purple and scarlet
and decked with gold and precious stones and pearls and drinking

the blood of the saints from a golden cup, and by this time
I'm talking too much the way I always do when I get nervous
and try to be interesting and make people laugh or at least
think I'm not a complete dolt, which,
of course, they do, so I say, "There's a lot of stuff out there that looks

like something else, but you don't resemble anything!"
and the beast says, "There are seven kings. Five have fallen.
One on his throne, one not yet come," and I say, "That's Kool
and the Gang with me; no rush, right?"
and he lifts one of his arms as though to backhand me, and I duck,

and he says, "I givin to great and small, rich
and poor, free and bond. I makin a mark on their hand
or on their forehead, and no man buyin or sellin save he have
the mark or the name of the beast or the number
of his name," and I say, "See, I don't get that part at all" and even make

the goes-right-over-my-head sign and then, "Your dragon
have a name? How about the lady?" and the beast says,
"The Dragon givin power unto me. The waters around me
are peoples and multitudes and nations
and tongues. And they hatin the Whore and makin her desolate

and naked and eatin her flesh and burnin her with fire,"
and I say, "Jesus is going to kick your ass, you know,"
and the beast throws all his heads back and lets out
this ungodly roar and stamps
my sand fort to smithereens and grabs the dragon and the woman

and does a forward roll into the waves and disappears
with a lot of splashing and dragon and whore noises,
and when I get to my feet again and wipe the water
and the sand out of my eyes, I see
my mother-in-law heading my way, and she has a hot dog in each hand,

and I say, "I'm really not hungry," and she says, "I know,
but I thought your friend might want one," and I say, "What friend?"
and she says, "That guy you were talking to, the older guy.
A little stooped, but kindly. Had a sweet smile.
Nice dog, too. I don't know about that woman, though. What'd you two

talk about?" and I say, "Oh, you know, the usual stuff.
Religion, mostly," and take a bite out of my hot dog,
and she says, "Nothing to talk about there. Only one way
to heaven," and I say, "I'm sure you're right
about that," and the water is almost calm now, a little choppy, maybe,

and she says, "You want some chips? I got you
some chips," and there's a little splash way out toward the horizon,
and she says, "What the h-e-double-toothpicks is that?"
and I start to say, "The beast that was
and is not and yet is" but instead say, "Big fish, maybe?" and look

at where my fort used to be as she waves her hand in front
of her face and says, "Phew, somebody passed air.
Did you pass air?" and I say, "Naw, I think it's brimstone"
and then "We should get our stuff together, I'm not
sure it's safe here," and she says, "What do you mean? It's a perfect day,"

so I sit back down and think, She's right, it's beautiful
out here, and I'm lucky to have this old lady in my life who loves
me and who gave me her daughter to love, and this is a great hot dog,
and I didn't even have to pay for it. Still, to have
a mouth that speaks great things in the slaughter and a head wounded

unto death but the deadly wound healed . . . who wouldn't
want dominion over all earthly things? And just then
my mother-in-law says, "What in the world are you talking about
now?" and I say, "Oops, did I say that out loud?"
but at the same time I'm thinking, Who wouldn't want to be that beast.

HORRIBLE THINGS MAY BE TRUE

Woman I know steps off the curb, and snap goes her leg
in two places—okay, snap, snap—and wooosh
goes her phone, out of reach. Just then the neighbor
steps out for a smoke and hears her scream
and rushes over and calls 911 and puts his jacket
under her head and lights up. Thank god for smokers!
It's a mistake to think that what we know is all there

is to it: "Horrible things may be true," says 13th-century
physician Ibn al-Nafis, "and familiar and praised things
may prove to be lies." Some truths we hold to be
self-evident: when asked the difference between sex
and love, Ornette Coleman said, "Well, you're not
always sure you're in love. But when you're having
sex, there's really no mistaking it." Yet others

are the fig newtons of our imagination, as when
an elderly lady of my acquaintance tells her daughter
that she is certain the Germans have planted a spy
among her round-the-clock sitters, and the daughter
says, "Mom, Sheniqua is *not* a German agent."
Speaking of which, wars are bad for the population
in general, but they are good for meteorologists:

there were 300 government weather-watchers
in 1939, 7000 in 1945 because generals need to know
if there's going to be mud tomorrow or not,
pilots if they have to fly through fog or moonlight.
War's also good for English departments: "U.S.
Literature since 1865," etc. Other than that,
who's for war? Not me! Myself, I would be pensive

and laborious: when Sherlock Holmes comes out
of retirement as a beekeeper, he shows Watson
his *Practical Handbook of Bee Culture,* "the fruit
of pensive nights and laborious days
when I watched the little working gangs as once I watched
the criminal world of London." Oh, and thankful,
too: for the man who stepped outside that night

and the wife who made him do so, for smokers
and for people who hate smoke. For dappled things,
for dawn-drawn Ford Falcons, for the whole kitten
caboodle I say *O wonderful, wonderful,* as Celia
does in *As You Like It* as she sees Rosalind dressed
as a man, *and most wonderful wonderful, and yet
again wonderful, and after that, out of all hooping!*

NOTES

If these poems work, they work best when they move the way the mind does. As people do when they're trying to figure out their day or plan a trip or decide what to have for dinner, I tend to start with a small thought, watch it snowball into something beyond itself, and, after a couple of minutes, do my best to bring everything together and make something that'll stand on its own.

Over the years, I've tried to learn as much as I can from the masters: Dante, Whitman, and especially Shakespeare. But my workshop would be a lot lonelier without the presence of innumerable others, at least some of whom I'd like to thank here.

"The Voice in the Other Room"

The reference to Cole Porter and the images that follow it are from the best essay I've ever read on repetition in poetry, which is by Marianne Boruch; it's called "Poetry's Over and Over" and appears in *In the Blue Pharmacy: Essays on Poetry and Other Transformations.*

"Roy G. Biv"

I wanted to convey the chewy variety of American poetry here, so I raided the file of blurbs I've written for poetry books in recent years. Many of the images in this poem come from lines of well-deserved praise I wrote earlier for these poets and their collections: Steve Fellner, *Blind Date with Cavafy;* Daniel Borzutzky, *The Ecstasy of Capitulation;* Mark Kraushaar, *Falling Brick Kills Local Man;* Richard Bausch, *These Extremes: Poems and Prose;* and Alan Michael Parker, *Elephants & Butterflies.*

"Senior Coffee"

In the course of a 4,000-mile train trip from St. Petersburg to Beijing, I had all the Russian greats with me (in an e-reader, of course), but along the way, I discovered Varlam Shalamov, whose *Kolyma Tales* recount almost photographically his years in the gulag. The list of things that step easily into poetry and make themselves at home there is based on a similar list in the best story in this collection, "Cherry Brandy," which imagines the final days of the poet Mandelstam as he lies dying in a prison camp, and the phrase "not for poetry but through poetry" is Shalamov's as well.

"Siberia"

Shalamov appears again in this poem; the sentences quoted here are from his memoir *The Fourth Vologda*. Shalamov's output was small, and his works are not easy to come by, but they're worth the search. Every sentence of his reads as though he worked it by hand, sighted down its length to make sure it was straight, and polished it until it was as perfect as anything can be on this earth.